The
WANT AD

AN ADOPTION STORY OF FAITH, HOPE AND LOVE

WANTED
Wanted a home for
2 small children;
Family must be Christian.

Bettye Faust Torbett Johnson

Dedication

To my loving husband of fifty-eight years, LaVoy.
He is the rock of my life and such an inspiration!
He has encouraged me and aided me every way
he could through this long journey of finding my
family and writing this book. Thank you, Honey.

Acknowledgments

Thank you to all of you who read my manuscript during the writing of this book. I would especially like to thank my friend Denise Waldrop for the hours she spent taking care of all my computer woes and giving suggestions and so much help along the way. My appreciation also goes to Iris Jackson for the laborious hours she spent proofreading and providing support. Thank you, thank you, to our daughter Grace for being so persistent about finding my family and for her constant encouragement.

Contents

Notes About Names

Since there are several spellings of names in this book, an explanation is needed. I was Betty June Faust before adoption. My biological family called me "June." My last name, Faust, was spelled with an "a"; however, somewhere along the way, my father changed the "*a*" in Faust to an "*o*": F<u>o</u>ust. Therefore, some of my siblings spell the name *Faust* and some spell it *Foust*. In his later years, my father resumed the original name Faust, as shown on his death certificate.

After adoption, I was Betty June Torbett, and they called me Betty June. In high school, I decided to put an "e" on Betty, because my adoptive mother was also named Betty Torbett. So, I became Bettye June Torbett. After college, I dropped the June and became Bettye Torbett. Then of course when I married, I became Bettye Torbett Johnson.

In this book, my birth father is known as "Father," and my adopted father is known as "Daddy." Because my birth mother passed away before I really knew her, I refer to her as my "birth mother" and my adopted mother as "Mother."

Prologue

By Grace Johnson Laster
(Third daughter of Bettye and LaVoy Johnson)

My siblings and I had always wondered about our Mom's biological family. Who were they? Where were they? How many were there? Did we have any uncles and aunts? What about cousins? Our family was somewhere out there.

Though Mom's adoptive family was very loving and kind, the mysteries of her original family lingered in the hearts and minds of all of us.

While my husband Jeff and I lived in Southwest Virginia, we visited the Knox County Court house in Tennessee in search of information on the William Hobert Faust family. We also visited the funeral homes in search of records bearing the Faust name. We spoke with merchants in the towns of Elizabethton (the town from which she was adopted) and Bristol with the hopes of finding clues about the Faust Family. These efforts bore no results.

A friend of ours at church excitedly shared that she had found her sister in an unusual way, and I immediately thought of my mom's family. Perhaps *this* might be the key to the Faust Family mystery!

This is my mom's story!

CHAPTER 1

WANTED
Wanted a home for
2 small children;
Family must be Christian.

THE BEGINNING

1989

I had just settled down in the family room to complete my lesson plans for the opening of the school year. The shrill sound of the telephone aroused me from my deep concentration. I answered very hurriedly, because I really didn't want to be disturbed.

"Hello!" I said.

In a slow, southern drawl, a voice on the other end of the phone said, "Hello, is this Bettye June Faust Torbett Johnson?"

I hesitated before answering, as only a very few people knew my full name. "Yes it is," I said.

"Well, this is Calvin Coolidge Faust, your brother." I was so excited I could hardly believe my ears. Was this really *my* brother? Was my life-long dream finally coming true?

"Oh," I thought, "the letter worked!"

1940

One sunny afternoon when I was about six years old, a friend, Patsy, and I were playing dolls in the front yard. I was the "mommy;" she was the "daddy," and we had two "babies."

While we were playing, Patsy suddenly looked over at me and said, "Your mommy got you from the mountains; she didn't even have you herself! You don't even have a real mommy and daddy."

Even though my feelings were badly hurt and I was bewildered, I continued to play and made up my mind not to let Patsy know how much her cruel words had upset me.

I didn't know exactly what she meant, but that evening as we "said our prayers," I told my mother what Patsy had said. With tears in her eyes, she explained that she could not have any children of her own but that God wanted her and Daddy to have a very special little girl, so He gave me to them.

She then further quieted my heart by saying, "Betty June, you are special because from all the other little boys and girls in the whole wide world, we chose you to be our very own!"

In the 1930's and 1940's, adoption was not spoken of openly. Mother told me not to talk about it and to act as though I was her own little girl. She explained that my real mother had passed away when I was a baby, and my father felt he could not take care of all the children by himself. She said that if anyone else said anything to me about it, to tell them just what she had explained: that my mother and daddy had picked me out from all the rest of the children. That was fine with me! Fortunately, it was not mentioned again—except occasionally—among family.

My adoptive mother, Cecil Elizabeth (Betty), was born in 1888 to John and Julia (Snyder) Zimmerman on a large farm in Mt. Olympus, Indiana. Her sister, Gertrude Leona, was born in 1892. Their father was a farmer and very proud of the bushels of corn, soybeans, wheat, rye, and oats which his farm produced each year. My grandfather liked to relate the story of his presence at the Snyder farm the day my grandmother was born. He went home and told his mother that the baby was so cute that someday, he was going to marry her And marry her he did—sixteen years later!

Unfortunately, my grandfather had a serious heart attack in his early forties, which resulted in his having to give up farming. He did not sell his farm but built a beautiful home at 508 South Seminary Street in Princeton, Indiana, and moved the family there.

Shortly thereafter, oil was discovered on the farm—a blessing from the Lord—which provided for him and his family for their entire lifetime, including college educations for both daughters, who graduated from Valparaiso University in Valparaiso, Indiana, with majors in Home Economics.

Following their graduation, Betty and Gertrude began teaching at Boaz Seminary in Boaz, Alabama, a school commissioned by the Methodist Episcopal Church and the oldest school in Alabama. (It is now known as Snead State Community College.) Betty taught the sewing courses, and Gertrude taught the culinary courses. Several years into their teaching careers, the brother of one of Betty's colleagues, Roscoe Torbett, came to visit and was introduced to Betty. One visit turned into two...then three... and then four. Betty and Roscoe fell in love and were married on Thanksgiving Day, November 28, 1929.

Betty and Roscoe very much wanted a child and knew they had the means to provide for a family, so they were heartbroken to learn that they would be unable to have children. They had so much love to give, and they seriously talked about adopting a child who needed a home.

One day while reading the newspaper, Betty read the following ad:

"Wanted: a home for two small children; family must be Christian."

Betty's sister, Gertrude, and their mother were visiting for the summer. After discussing this that evening, Betty and Roscoe decided it would be good to respond to the ad of William Hobert Faust. Shortly, a reply came from my father.

FAUST JEWELRY CO.
Expert Watch & Jewelry Repairing
DON'T TAKE CHANCES, BRING IT TO US
418 ELK AVE. ELIZABETHTON, TENN.

June 6, 1938

Mrs.R.R.Torbett
519 Ga. Ave.
Bristol, Tenn.

Dear Mrs.Torbett

Just Recived your Letter in regard to My
Children, I will first gave you a little history of our
family, My Wife died a little over three years ago.
Since that time I have been having a time trying to raise
the Children as they should be, and at the same time run
a Business.
I have One little Girl three-years of age, She was a little
Baby at the Time her Mother DEATH.

The Next Little Girl is five years of age.
I am in The Jewelry Business,.
I would like to bring the Little Girls to see You any time
you write Me and tell me the Date you would want me to bring
them.

Yours Truly,
William H. Faust
WILLIAM H.FAUST

Letter to Mrs. R. R. Torbett, June 6, 1938

Since Betty and Gertrude felt it would be help-
ful if they became acquainted with the children's
background, they arranged to go to see the girls
the following week.

CHAPTER 2

WANTED
Wanted a home for
2 small children;
Family must be Christian.

The Adoption

After all these years, I remember well that beautiful June afternoon in 1938. My sister Juanita and I had been playing in the yard when my oldest sister, Stella, called us and told us we had to take a bath. We didn't want to stop our playing and couldn't understand why we had to take a bath in the middle of the day. She said some ladies were coming to see us. Stella had filled a washtub with water which had been warmed by the sun. I remember she gave us very good baths and had us put on our best clothes.

As Betty and Gertrude approached the house in Elizabethton, Tennessee, they were amazed to see a very small two-bedroom clapboard house nestled in a group of trees. (All the children slept in one tiny bedroom.) There were several children playing around in the dirt yard. My father told the ladies again that his wife had passed away about three years ago—when I was nine months old. He explained that he had remarried, that they had another child, and that his new wife was overwhelmed at taking care of eight children. He said he also thought that the little girls would have a much better life with someone who could give them more time and attention than he could.

Betty explained to him that since she and her husband were older than most parents, they did not feel they could take both children. My father was pleased to find a new home for even one of us and said he wanted to be able to come to see me at least once a month to be sure I was okay. Betty told him he could come only as a friend of the family—not as my father—to which he readily agreed because he said my welfare was his only concern. My new parents were to have thirty days to see how I adjusted to life without my family and to have me checked thoroughly by a doctor.

After talking more than an hour to my father and getting acquainted with my sister and me, the ladies left, taking only me with them. (Betty, about to become my new mother, later told me it was my big brown eyes and very dark shiny hair that caused her to choose me.)

A presentation

It is contracted and agreed that Betty June Faust will remain in the custody of Mr & Mrs R.R. Torbett for a period of 30 days at which time it will be decided as to whether or not she will be adopted into the family of R.R. Torbett with all privaleges and core under due process governing such adoption.

Signed William H. Faust
Father of Betty June

At Elizabethton Tenn

June 12th 1938

Witnessed
Signed _____

FAUST JEWELRY CO.
Expert Watch & Jewelry Repairing
DON'T TAKE CHANCES, BRING IT TO US
418 ELK AVE.   ELIZABETHTON, TENN.

Presentation

Even though Stella had dressed me in the very best clothes I had, Mother stopped at King's Department store on the way to my new home to purchase new underwear, a dress, and shoes, because, as she told me later, she did not want the neighbors to think she had gotten a "little rag-a-muffin."

My new home in Bristol, Tennessee, was totally opposite from my old home. It was a beautiful red-brick house with an indoor bathroom, a bathtub, shiny hardwood floors, and a telephone! I even remembered the telephone number; it was 1196-L.

My first memory was of my feet flying out from under me on the slippery floor.

The trip to the doctor revealed that I had rickets and would need a highly nutritious diet so that my bones would grow strong; other than that, I was just fine!

My New Home with Mother and Daddy

We had three great meals every day. Almost immediately, I was taught how to set the table, help wash and dry dishes, and make my bed. Of course, I had a bedroom all to myself and lots of toys to play with.

Regarding my father's visits, I only remember a man coming to the house and talking with Mother. (She told me later that I had acted as though I didn't even know him.) He asked Mother to write him once a year to let him know how I was doing and to send a recent picture. Because I had been extremely quiet since joining my new family, Mother asked my father if I could talk.

His prompt response was, "Oh yes, Mrs. Torbett; she talks a lot!"

The clearest memory I have of my father was when I was very ill with something like the flu, and he made a little pallet on the hearth for me and kept me there all night, putting coal in the fire to keep it going and wiping my very hot forehead with a cool cloth. (Years later, after I was married, a dentist asked if I had ever had a high fever when I was very young. He explained that he could see fever lines on my teeth—a condition caused by extremely high fever at a very young age.) Again, I wondered about my family and exactly how I had been raised prior to my adoption.

When the thirty-day "trial period" was almost up, my new daddy wrote the following letter to my father.

Bristol, Tennessee
July 9th, 1938.

Mr. William H. Faust
Elizabethton, Tenn.

Dear Sir;

Betty June seems well satisfied in our home
and has adapted herself to the new surroundings.

We expect to file adoption papers during the
coming week, if there are no objections and satisfactory
with all concerned. This will be handled by our attorney
here and we expect to present it to Judge Bandy at Bristol
(Tenn. Courthouse) July 15th. Official notice will no doubt
be given you before certification is made.

If you wish to communicate with us before this
is done, you will please handle immediately.

Yours truly

R. R. Torbett

#519 Georgia Ave.
Bristol, Tenn.
Telephone 1196-L

COPY

To Mr. Faust from Mr. Torbett, July 9, 1938

My birth father replied immediately.

William H. Faust
418 Elk Ave.
Elizabethton, Tenn.

July 12, 1938

MR.R.E.Torbett
519 Georgia Ave.
Bristol, Tennessee

Dear Sir;

I recived your letter of July 9,1938
In regard to The adoption of my child, Betty June Faust.
as you no doubt know,,When a Child is adopted the natural
parents are relieved of all duties towards(him)or her in
return for which they forfeit all their rights in the Child.
(In Court,)

IT was aggred that I would have the right to Visit your family
at any time I may Desire.But only as a Friend of the Family.,

I would want this in a WRITEN AGGREMENT, before the adoption
papers go to Court,,as to references I have give you some on
my self, So for I have not recieved any from You;
To-day is the day you were to go over the Matter with ME.

You were to Come to Elizabethton,(July 12,1938)

Mr.Torbett Please dont think that I want to be out of reasons
about this," I want to adopt her to you onlY under these
conditions specified in this Letter.

I will come to Bristol,Tenn. any time you want me to COME.;
as I am very anxious to do this adoption right;

Yours Truly,

William H. Faust

WILLIAM H.FAUST

P.S.
    Mr.Torbett as you no doubt remember me telling you
and your Wife that I would not Adopt Betty June Faust
to any one that would not give ME THE RIGHT TO COME SEE
HER. Any time I Wanted to Come.,

To Mr. Torbett from Mr. Faust, July 12, 1938

A special delivery letter from my daddy was sent the next day.

Finally, on July 22, 1938, the Decree of Adoption was signed in the County Court of Sullivan County, Tennessee.

At last, at age four, I was Betty June Torbett!

CHAPTER 3

WANTED
Wanted a home for
2 small children;
Family must be Christian.

Some Childhood Memories

My new mother and Aunt Gertrude treated me like a china doll. They took care of all my needs and spent hours playing with me. A big concern of theirs was that I did not talk or really show much emotion. One day while I was playing Chinese checkers with Aunt Gertrude, a marble fell on the floor, and we were both down on the floor looking for it.

I saw the marble across the room, and I said, "Thar 'tis!"

Aunt Gertrude jumped up and ran into the kitchen where Mother was and said, "Betty June said, 'Thar 'tis.'"

Mother said, "What kind of talk is that?"

It did not take me long to use my "mountain talk," and Mother thought it most important that I learn to speak correctly. Every day when she read Bible stories to me, she would also read other passages from the Bible and help me memorize the Scriptures and pronounce the words correctly. She began with the Christmas story in

Luke chapter two. Little did I know what she had in mind for me!

Mother made all my clothes, using smocking, embroidery, cross-stitching, and all kinds of rick-rack and lace. As soon as my shiny dark brown hair was long enough, she gave me a permanent. She even had a professional photographer come to our house to take pictures of me!

Betty June with straight hair

Betty June with curly hair

She was fulfilling her dream of being a mother. She was also an excellent cook; however, when Aunt Gertrude and Grandmother were there in the summertime, they did most of the cooking, so she could spend time with me.

Each day would begin with a nourishing breakfast. Then, Mother would take Daddy to work. Until I started school, I usually went with them. Daddy would tell me stories about trains and things he did at work. He was called a store-keeper. His job involved taking care of a large train depot and warehouse. After Mother got the evening meal prepared, we would make the trip back to pick up Daddy from work.

She would let me go up to Daddy's office, and he would walk with me back to the car, having me speak to each of the men whom we passed.

He would always tell me their names, and I would say, "Hello, Mr. Brown."

I remember on one occasion, when I momentarily turned my head and did not speak to the man, Daddy had said was Mr. Jackson.

Immediately he said, "Why didn't you speak to him?"

I said, "Because he was dirty," and I turned up my nose.

Daddy let me know in no uncertain terms that Mr. Jackson was one of his best mechanics, and that he worked on big, dirty engines. He explained that just because he was dirty from hard labor, that didn't change who he was. He said that I should never frown on anyone just because they are dirty. I learned a very important lesson that day that has served me well throughout the years.

On the way to and from Daddy's work, I always noticed a very large house with lots of children playing in the yard and asked Mother what that house was and who lived there. She explained that it was an orphanage where little girls and boys who had no home stayed. I always felt so sorry for them and wished I could do something to help make them happy!

Upon returning home, I would set the table, and Mother would put the dinner on the table. My parents taught me several blessings, and each evening, I would "say grace" before we ate.

In the evening, Daddy was usually the center of attention. We would listen to the news together and then maybe to a radio program.

Mother and Daddy

Daddy would read the paper, and sometimes we would go for a walk. In warm weather, we would sit on the beautiful front porch, and I would run around the yard catching lightning bugs.

One evening, I caught a large bumble bee instead! Daddy grabbed me in his arms, ran inside, dumped out his pipe (he smoked very rarely), and put the tobacco on the bee sting. Then he sat and held me until it quit hurting. When it was time for bed, he would always come with Mother to tuck me in.

The last word from my father was a letter to Daddy on December 14, 1938, inquiring about me. He also sent a Christmas gift at that time, but I do not remember what it was. In fact, I am not sure my mother ever gave it to me.

The following is Daddy's reply to my father's letter:

Bristol, Tenn.
Dec. 20th, 1938

Mr. William H. Faust
Elizabethton, Tenn.

Dear Sir;

       I am in receipt of your letter of Dec. 14th, and the
package you sent.

       I am inclosing a picture of Betty June. Her health is
good and she is learning to count and spell. Your request has
been considered, and you may arrange to come to my home, Monday
Dec. 26th, abot 3 P M. for a short visit. It must be understood
that the name (Faust) or relatives are to be mentioned in her
presence, or anything that would identify the connection. This
may not be done in the future as it our desire that the decision
of the Court be adhered to.

       If the above time is not convenient for you, you may
arrange an appointment with us.

       Wishing you all a Merry Christmas and a Happy New
Year, I am,

             Yours truly

             R. R. Torbett

#519 Ga. Ave.
Bristol, Tenn.

To Mr. Faust from Mr. Torbett, December 20, 1938

I do not think my father came to visit—even though Daddy had said he could.

My first Christmas with my new parents, we rode a big black train to Princeton, Indiana, to my grandmother's and Aunt Gertrude's house. Mother could hardly wait to show me off to all her friends. That is when my public speaking began! I had memorized the Christmas story, Luke 2:1–11, which I gave as the "devotional" for several Sunday school classes and other church groups for their Christmas parties. I always closed with a prayer, and of course, my mother and Aunt Gertrude beamed from ear to ear!

I do not remember ever going to church before I was adopted; however, in later years when I found my birth family, my brothers told me some nice people would come by our house and take us to church. They said my birth mother was usually sick, and our father just didn't go.

My new home brought a drastic change in my lifestyle. On Sunday, Mother would dress me in my very best clothes, and we would go to Sunday school and church at the State Street Methodist Church. This church was on the main street in Bristol, which is located on the state line dividing Tennessee and Virginia. This was very fascinating to me. It was a very beautiful, large, and formal church. It was in this church that I went forward when I was about eight years old and joined the church. I trusted the Lord as my Savior later.

In the afternoons, Mother would write a letter to her mother and her sister who lived in the old home place in Princeton, Indiana. After the letter was complete, Daddy and I would go for a walk into town to the drugstore to mail the letter. We would usually just talk or sing along the way. Of course, the trip would always end with a chocolate milkshake or a chocolate ice cream cone!

When I was six, I began school at Fairmount Elementary School, just a few blocks from our house. Mother always walked with me to the end of our block and then stood and watched to be certain I arrived safely at school. I enjoyed going to school and being with other children. My first-grade teacher was Miss Hilton, and I thought she was beautiful. I wanted to be a teacher just like her.

I had my tonsils out the summer after first grade. Back then, tonsils were taken out in the doctor's office. My most vivid recollection is eating crushed ice and ice cream after the procedure.

CHAPTER 4

WANTED

Wanted a home for
2 small children;
Family must be Christian.

Lessons Learned Early in Life

I continued to be so interested in the "big house" we passed on the way to pick up Daddy that Mother decided to do something about it. We went to the home and asked if we could bring two or three little girls home with us to have a little party with me. They approved, and so the summer parties began. Three or four times each summer, we would have parties for different children at the orphanage. At the end of the summer, Mother would bake cupcakes, and we would go to the orphanage and have fun with the children my age.

This evolved into our having young Christmas guests in our home. We would begin in the summer to collect toys that were still good—but maybe needed a little repair—and put them in the basement. There were always big dolls, a tricycle and scooter, doll furniture, books and games, and other things I had used the previous year.

On Saturday mornings, Daddy and I would go to the basement and begin repairing, painting, and shining up the toys. Then we would go to the orphanage and choose a little girl to bring home with us for a couple of days: either the week before Christmas (if we were going to Grandmother's for Christmas) or the twenty-third through the twenty-fifth (if we were going to be home for Christmas). This continued until I was eight or nine years of age. What wonderful memories those were for me! This ingrained into me the joy of giving and loving those who had much less than I.

I remember very well when we went to mail the Sunday letter on December 7, 1941; I was seven years old.

As we approached the drugstore, boys seemed to be everywhere with sandwich boards over their shoulders and proclaiming, "*Extra! Extra!*" Daddy said Pearl Harbor had been bombed by the Japanese, and we were at war. Everybody was extremely sad and talking very excitedly. Of course, I had no idea what he was talking about, but when we didn't sing on the way home, I knew it was bad!

I also remember his taking me to the train depot in downtown Bristol one bright, sunny Saturday morning. There was a huge blue whale on display on two open flatcars. Daddy told me all about whales and how this one was the biggest whale God had made, and it swam in the Pacific Ocean. There was a very small platform on one side of the whale, and I remember going up the stairs to touch the whale; it was so slimy!

Daddy had two sisters, Aunt Gertie and Aunt Dimple, who lived in Bristol also. They both worked, but we would see them quite often. Aunt Gertie was the office manager of Ford Motor Company, and Daddy would take me there—as he said—"just to show me off."

I loved these aunts dearly; they treated me like a queen. When Mother and Daddy went out of town, I stayed with them. One of the favorite things I remember their doing was to seat me at their dressing table in the bedroom and put all kind of creams and makeup on my face.

They polished my nails and I thought I was "big stuff." I was not aware of it at the time, but Aunt Gertie was purchasing a war bond for me on each of my birthdays and putting them in her safe deposit box. When she passed away, of course, they were given to me. I always think this is another way God was taking care of us. It came at a time in our married life when we really needed extra money for our family.

Sometimes when I needed to be punished, Mother would send me to my room, and I would entertain myself by: reading a book, playing "family" with my dolls, tearing up paper to make "meals" for the family, or just singing. Mother said she felt like even when she punished me, I still had lots of fun, so I was never really punished!

When I was ten, Mother and Daddy sold our house and purchased a new home out in the country so that Mother could have a Victory garden and do more canning. However, just before we were planning to move, Daddy became very ill, which prevented our moving.

The new owners of our house were in no rush to move and very kindly let us stay there as long as necessary. Mother took care of Daddy at home until he needed more skilled care and had to be moved to the Veterans Hospital in Arlington, Virginia. Only a few days later, he passed away on Thanksgiving Day—their fifteenth wedding anniversary.

His death certificate states that he starved to death, because he could not swallow. Of course, there were no feeding tubes back then, so there was no way to give him nourishment. We assume he had cancer of the esophagus or some kind of blockage in his throat.

Daddy lay in state in our living room; his funeral was there also. We went by train to Princeton, Indiana, for his burial and returned to Bristol the day after the burial. Mother began packing immediately: she was moving back to her old home place where she grew up and where Aunt Gertrude and Grandmother still lived.

After the movers came, we prepared for our eight hundred-mile trip back to Indiana. I will never forget that frightful drive in almost constant snow over the mountainous roads. As I recall, we spent three nights in hotels, as there were no motels in those days.

In each place we stayed, the beautiful Christmas decorations helped a little to take away our sadness over losing Daddy. In the evenings, many people came down to the lobby to hear the weather report on the radio. If anyone could play the piano, we sang Christmas carols. It seemed to help my mother to be around other people. At the time, I was collecting Christmas candles: little snowmen, Santas, Christmas trees, and candy canes. Mother made sure I looked for them and let me purchase whatever I wanted.

We had a very sad Christmas that year—our first one without Daddy—but Mother had many friends, and of course, Grandmother and Aunt Gertrude comforted and supported us.

CHAPTER 5

WANTED
Wanted a home for
2 small children;
Family must be Christian.

MY HOME IN INDIANA

Going into a new school in the middle of the year was difficult for me. Franklin Elementary School was five or six blocks from my home, and of course, I walked to school every day.

The teachers were all very nice, but it seemed as though the classes were more difficult. I remember making a *C* in math the first grading period, and Mother was really upset. She went to the school and talked with my teacher. Immediately, we began working at home on math, math, and *more* math! It didn't take long for me to realize the importance of a good education. Soon, I began enjoying the other students. Some of the friends I made there became lifelong friends.

My seventh and eighth grades were at Lowell Jr. High, which was eleven or twelve blocks away and this again became my daily exercise. I made more friends, and I remember my Jr. High years as good ones. I became very active in Girl Scouts and 4-H and Methodist Youth Fellowship at my church. These three organizations, because of their requirements and high expectations of each member, helped me to maximize my abilities and strengthened me in many areas. I will always cherish the memories of all the things learned during those years.

Then came high school—oh, what wonderful memories I have. Our class was one of a kind. To this day, I still have contact with my classmates! They are a wonderful, wholesome group who have accomplished much in their lives.

At our forty-year class reunion, I told the story of my adoption. My classmates did not know I had been adopted. They were quite interested in how finding my family came about, and they asked many questions.

After the program, one of my classmates said to me, "You don't know how relieved I am that you told that story tonight!"

When I asked what he meant by that, he explained, "When we were in high school, I asked my mother why your mother was so much older than all the other parents. She wouldn't answer me for a long time. I just couldn't figure it out, but finally she said, 'I will tell you, but if you tell any-one—believe me—you will be sorry!' So I never told anyone. You knew my mom, and believe me, you know I would have been *very* sorry!"

He continued by saying, "Coming to the reun-ion, I knew I would see you, and I asked my wife if she thought you knew you were adopted. Naturally, she didn't know, so I told her I thought I should have a heart-to-heart talk with you and be sure you knew. I thought it would be terri-ble for you to live your whole life and not know where you came from!"

We had a good laugh about this, but it just shows the concern we had for our fellow classmates.

In high school, I took a business course, because I really didn't feel I would have the funds to go to college. My mother was living on a pension from the Norfolk and Western Railroad (where my daddy had worked). We had experienced a drought on the farm for the past four or five years, and the crops were poor. The only other source of income she had was from the oil wells on the farm—which had been quite large and supplied the whole family for years—but they were also drying up. So I thought if I could be equipped to take a job right out of high school, I could help her and hopefully save some money for college. So, this was the path I had chosen.

The Lord was good, and immediately after graduation, I found a job as the secretary for the personnel director at Chrysler Corporation in Evansville, Indiana, about twenty-five miles away. I found a ride so that I could live at home and save money; however, my mother insisted on my paying a little rent so I could get used to living away from home.

Mother had told me that years before, she and Aunt Gertrude had invested in a little college in Florida called Bob Jones College. The college had since moved to Greenville, South Carolina. She contacted them and asked to cash out the bonds, because she was a widow and needed the money for her daughter. The school told her that the bonds had been cashed out years before, and that they could not return the money now, but they explained they would apply the money to her daughter's account if she came to Bob Jones when she was ready for college.

In the fall of 1953, I rode to Greenville, South Carolina, on the train by myself, because I could ride free of charge since my daddy had been an employee. I had never visited the school before, and it seemed strange to be among so many people I had never met.

Everyone was so kind and friendly; it did not take long to fall in love with my new surroundings. I began working in the office immediately. The second semester, I had a full work-loan scholarship, which meant that I worked several hours a day and took a smaller load of classes. I wanted to finish in four years, so I also took correspondence courses to replace the classes I did not take at Bob Jones.

It was at Bob Jones University that I met and married the love of my life, LaVoy Johnson, in 1955.

Our meeting and subsequent marriage reminds me of the famous saying of Dr. Bob Jones, Sr., "You don't find happiness looking for it; you find happiness on the road of duty!"

After we married, I finished my Elementary Education degree while he finished an advanced degree. We graduated together in 1957.

After graduation, we joined the Campus Crusade Ministry. As we traveled across the country to California, I often wondered if we were passing the homes of any of my siblings. Our first assignment was at Oklahoma University.

Again I wondered, "Is my family here?"

We had a bittersweet stay in Oklahoma; our first son, David, was stillborn. We had been in Norman, Oklahoma, only four months, and of course, most of our acquaintances were students and the staff of Campus Crusade. It was impossible for either of our families to come to Oklahoma; so basically, we were alone in this very sad time in our lives. But God's grace was certainly sufficient for us at that time! We were strengthened spiritually and emotionally.

God provided a doctor who gave us a bill marked, "paid in full." So we had a hospital bill that cost nothing, and a funeral and burial which were covered by an insurance policy that we had taken out only two months before! I always felt as though we had abandoned our son in Oklahoma, because we were moved to Michigan to begin the work at Michigan State University.

Fifty years later, we were blessed through our children, who insisted we return to Oklahoma to have a formal service at David's grave site. We could not purchase a tombstone at the time of his death, and our children had a beautiful stone put in place—made from Georgia marble. Jeff Laster, our son-in-law, gave the message, and our children sang for the service. It was an experience we will never forget, and it gave us closure to a very sad time in our lives.

It was also in Oklahoma that we were blessed by the arrival of our first daughter, Beth. What a blessing she has been!

CHAPTER 6

WANTED
Wanted a home for
2 small children;
Family must be Christian.

THE SEARCH

Through the years, I had often wondered about my biological family; however, two reasons caused me to begin to look for them in earnest:

- When I began to have children, the doctors always asked me about my medical history; and of course, I knew nothing about my biological family's health.
- I determined to find my brothers and sisters and know for sure about their salvation.

One day at church, our pastor, Dr. Curtis Hutson, asked if we knew for sure we were going to Heaven. I was positive I was; I had accepted the Lord as my Savior when I was twelve years old, and I knew for sure I was going to spend eternity with the Lord.

The next question was: "How about your family? Do you know for sure your family is going to Heaven?"

Again, I knew my husband and children had all accepted the Lord, but a little voice said to me, "What about your brothers and sisters?"

The reason I had not looked for my family sooner was because I did not want to give my mother and Aunt Gertrude any cause for pain, and I didn't want them to feel I didn't appreciate all the sacrifices they had made for me.

I made only a few calls and sent a story to the Bristol Herald explaining that I was looking for my family and asking anyone who might know the whereabouts of any of my family to contact me. After receiving no responses, I pushed these thoughts aside and decided I should wait until after my adopted mother had passed away.

After she died in 1972, my search began in earnest. She had left me an envelope which contained my biological father's and mother's names and a few pictures as well as some of the letters I have included in this book.

My Birth Father

My brother, Paul and sister, Stella

Mother had written to my birth father once a year at Christmas as she had promised. When I was a junior in high school, her letter was returned. She assumed he had passed away or was no longer concerned about me. Therefore, it had been years since there had been any correspondence. I remembered three siblings' names: Paul (the oldest), Stella Mae (the oldest girl who tried to take care of us when my mother died), and Juanita (who was my constant playmate and just three years older than I).

With these names and the knowledge that they lived in Tennessee at the time of my adoption, I began to look earnestly for my family. I joined several adoption agencies and searched the US Census Records. Here, I found that William H. Foust was the second son born to Oliver and Sarah Smith Foust on January 2, 1898. But how would that help me, and where was he now? I searched the Mormon Church records, the Social Security Administration, and the U S Army, because one of the pictures showed my brother, Paul, in an Army uniform. I was told if I knew their birth dates or if I had Paul's Army Serial number or Stella or Juanita's married names (assuming they were married), they could help me; otherwise, they could not. Of course, I did not have that information.

Grace, my youngest daughter who was married and lived in Virginia, asked me to send her all the information I had and said that she and her husband, Jeff, would go to Bristol and the surrounding areas and search the records for me. This they did: making many, many phone calls, writing letters, and going personally to check things out. All of this was to no avail.

The next summer, LaVoy and I decided to go to Elizabethton and Bristol, Tennessee, to search all the places they hadn't: birth and death records at the courthouse, the retirement homes, cemeteries, and funeral homes. We found the building where my father's jewelry store had been, and the people there remembered him but had no information about him or the family.

By 1989, I was about ready to give up when my daughter Grace called and said, "Mom, a friend of mine wrote a letter to her sister who had been adopted and sent it to the Social Security Administration, and they delivered it for her. It took a while, but she did find her sister that way. Why don't you try that?"

I was beginning my twenty-second year of teaching, and the school year was just opening. I told her I couldn't spend any more time on the search at the present time. We had spent most of the summer doing what I thought was one final search.

Grace said, "Would you mind if I wrote the letters as if they were from you?"

I said, "Absolutely not; that would be wonderful."

She said, "Okay, I will write them *for* you!"

She reminded me that it could take possibly two or three months to receive a reply, but hopefully, we would all be together by Christmas.

I was very disappointed that our one last final effort had not been successful, but I determined to put all my efforts into getting the new school year off to a good start. Actually, I don't think I thought about it again until September ninth, only two weeks after Grace had said she would write to the Social Security Administration. On that day the following letter came in the mail.

Stella Mae Faust Petersen
101 Moreno Crt.
Pensacola, Fl. 32507

Dear Stella Mae,   8-27-89

    I am your youngest sister, June. To my understanding, I was adopted out of the Faust family at the age of four due to our mother's death and our father's inability to care for his youngest children and operate his jewelry store in Elizabethton, Tenn.

    Over the years I have wondered about my natural family and long to be reunited with them. Our brother's names that I recall are Paul and Dan. I also recall a sister named Juanita who was placed up for adoption the same time I was.

    My natural parents names are: William Hubert Faust married to Luella Micklin Faust in Knox County, Tenn. (1918).

    I greatly desire to locate you and hope to hear from you very soon. Please call me at your earliest convenience. My phone number is: 404-482-7172. My address is: 1074 Rock Chapel Road Lithonia, Georgia 30058

          Sincerely,
          Bettye June Faust T. Johnson

Letter to Stella from Grace

DEPARTMENT OF HEALTH & HUMAN SERVICES

Social Security Administration
Poff Federal Building
CS 1000
Roanoke, Va. 24005

Refer to:

Phone: 703 982-6188

September 7, 1989

Mrs. B. June Faust Johnson
1074 Rock Chapel Rd.
Lithonia, Ga. 30058

Dear Mrs. Johnson:

We have received your request to forward letters to your two missing
sisters.

We will search our records to determine if we have an address for
these people. If an address is located, we will attempt to forward
your letters. If an address is not located we can take no further
action nor can we notify you of this fact. Therefore, we cannot
assure you that your letter will be delivered or that you will receive
a reply. In any event, we cannot forward a second letter.

Sincerely yours,

M. R. Franklin

M. R. Franklin
Service Representative

Dear Mrs. Petersen:

We are enclosing a letter which Mrs. Bettye June Faust Johnson has
asked us to forward to you.

Because of the circumstances, we agreed to forward the letter.
However, we have not revealed your address, and cannot disclose
whether the letter has been delivered. You are free, therefore,
to reply or not as you choose. You need not notify us of your
decision.

Sincerely yours

M. R. Franklin

M. R. Franklin
Service Representative

Enclosure:

Letter from Social Security to Bettye

Letter from Social Security to Stella

They informed me that they had received my letter, and they would look for my siblings; however, they could not give me their addresses nor could they let me know if indeed they ever found them. They informed me that any correspondence must come to me directly from my brothers or sisters if they wanted to contact me. I thought, would they call? Would they write?

Feeling disappointed again, I put the letter on the coffee table and settled down on the couch to finish my lesson plans when the phone rang.

CHAPTER 7

WANTED
Wanted a home for
2 small children;
Family must be Christian.

TEN OF US

This brings me back to the male voice that said, "Is this Bettye June Faust Torbett Johnson?"

Not believing my ears, I hesitantly said, "Yes."

I knew the letter had been received; it had to be someone from my family, because no one else would know my biological name as well as my maiden name and married name.

He said, "This is Calvin Coolidge Faust: your brother!"

I replied, "I didn't know I had a brother named Calvin."

He then questioned, "Are you sitting down?"

When I replied in the affirmative, he said, "Well, there are *ten* of us!"

Needless to say, by this time, I was so excited that I called my husband to get on the phone and listen to the conversation so I wouldn't miss anything. My doubts as to who was on the other end of the line vanished when Calvin filled in the gaps of my family history and completed the pieces that had puzzled me throughout the years.

We spent about three hours on the phone—talking, laughing and crying. He gave me all the names, addresses, and phone numbers of all my other siblings and of our father's three sisters who were still living. Before we hung up, he made me promise to call them immediately. He said if I didn't call them by the next day, he would call them himself, because he couldn't keep this secret any longer!

He asked if I would be busy the next weekend, because he would like to fly up from Pensacola to bring me some family history and pictures. I said that would be wonderful, and he promised to send me his itinerary in the next day or so. He said he thought we should plan a reunion—perhaps for Thanksgiving. He said the whole family had not been together for over forty years, and it might take a miracle to get them all together, but he would certainly try. Even when our father passed away in 1974, those living on the West Coast went to the funeral in Texas, and those in the East went to a memorial service and burial in Tennessee. He was sorry he didn't have a recent picture, but he would include a couple of pictures so I could locate him easily at the airport.

Immediately after we hung up, I began calling my siblings. I called those on the East Coast first, and by the time I got to the ones on the West Coast, it was beginning to get late—even in their time zone! I was able to reach them all except one, who called me back shortly. My phone bill was astronomical, but it was worth every penny!

When I called Aunt Bertha, my father's sister in Sedona, Arizona, she cried and cried and said I just didn't know how long she had been praying that I would be found before she died. She expressed how upset she was when her brother, Hobert, had "given me away." She was thrilled to know we had a daughter, Pattye, who had a family and lived in Phoenix. She said, "Oh, I will make them my adopted grandchildren." I told her we were all trying to get together for a reunion on Thanksgiving Day, but that I was sure Pattye couldn't fly back to Atlanta, since she had just been here for a music conference. Immediately, Aunt Bertha said she would call Pattye and invite her and her family to spend Thanksgiving Day with her and her husband, Harry, since Pattye should definitely be with Faust family on the very important day of our reunion.

After Calvin called, I received a packet in the mail from him. He just sent a few facts about the family and a couple of pictures. He said he would be wearing khaki pants and a navy blue blazer when he came to see me. He said this should help me identify him at the airport.

As I looked at the picture, it was hard to grasp the idea that this was actually *MY* brother! Particularly in high school, I often wanted a "big brother," and to think, I had *four* of them! It was hard to sleep that week because of the anticipation of the visit from *my* brother.

Saturday, September 16, found LaVoy and me up very early to travel to the Atlanta airport. Calvin's plane was due at 8:30 a.m., and I certainly didn't want to be late. I wanted every minute I could have with my brother. As my luck would have it, there were three men who came off the plane with khaki pants and navy blazers.

Calvin and Bettye

When the first one came through the gate, I looked closely and thought, "That can't be my brother."

The second one didn't look like he would be in my family either, but when the third one came into the waiting room; I just knew it was Calvin.

We were both smiling from ear to ear—even with tears in our eyes—because we had at last found each other after fifty-one years.

When we finally settled down to get really acquainted, I looked at the five-inch stack of information he had brought with him. I always considered myself very organized, and I paid a lot of attention to details, but *wow*; I suddenly dropped that thought and realized that I didn't hold a candle to Calvin's organizational skills.

We went through the stack page by page. He had typed notes and had attached them to each document and picture. It was like going through the archives of our lives. Calvin told things about the family in such a picturesque way that I felt like I was actually with the family through the years.

We talked about our mother. He said she was a very meek and mild lady who never seemed to get too stressed about anything. He said she was sick quite often.

"Of course," he said, "any lady who had seven children by the time she was thirty-five would naturally be sick quite often!"

He showed me a copy of the last letter our mother had written to our father two months before she died.

It was difficult to read, so he translated it for me. It read:

January 15, 1935

Hobert, I hate to ask again, but I want you to send me some money today just as soon as you get this letter, as I am out of money. It takes so much, and I can hardly get by. I could not call as promised. What about getting a little coal? The people next door won't have any left. They are still there.

Send as much [money] as you can. I will try to get a little coal too. I hate it, because you will not get to come in to see the children. I was awful glad to see Paul last night. Be sure and send the money as I am out of coal completely. I call, but it didn't do any good much. Hope it will.

Luella

P.S. Will look for you Thursday morning.

He also had a copy of the last postcard our mother had written to my father: dated March 20, 1935, just ten days before she passed away. It read:

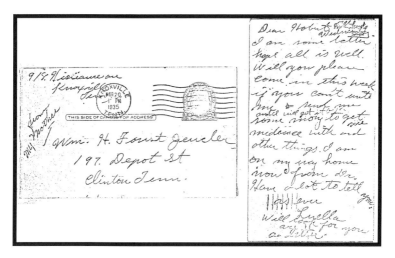

Postcard from my birth mother 10 days before she died

Dear Hobert,

I am some better. Hope all is well with you. Will you please come in this week? If you can't, write me and send me some money to get medicine with and other things. I am on my way home now from the doctor. Have a lot to tell you.

As ever,

Luella

Will look for you or a letter.

Calvin said it seemed as though our mother had some kind of disease or something, and that was what she wanted to tell him about. He said he remembered her crying a lot during those last few days before she passed away. Since she had to have much assistance from our grandparents and aunts to carry on the normal routine of caring for the seven children, our father moved the family into our grandparents' home in Clinton, Tennessee. This is the information Calvin gave me about her death:

Our mother had not improved after you were born. Her many trips to the doctor only verified the fact that her condition was becoming worse daily.

On Saturday morning, March 30, 1935, our mother was coming down the stairs to make another trip to the doctor when she missed her footing and fell down the long flight of stairs. Sherman, who had just come in from the yard, ran to his mother's side and called for his father to come quickly. As she lay white and still at the bottom of the steps, our father and his mother hovered over her, looking for some sign of life...but there was none. They gently carried her into the bedroom and sat sobbing as they waited for the doctor to arrive.

When the doctor came, he went into Mother's room. With our father by her side, the doctor said that Mother had broken her neck in the fall. He also said that Mother had been a very sick lady, and she probably fell because she got dizzy and could not hold on to the rail.

The children began rushing in from the yard after hearing all the commotion, and one by one, they sobbed as they hugged their mother—who had been such a loving, caring human being.

The days and nights that followed were so lonely, and you could be heard crying and calling, "Mama, Mama."

Shortly after our mother's death, our father moved the family back to Elizabethton, Tennessee, into a small, white clapboard house and returned to his jewelry store. Stella, who was almost eleven, took over the cooking and caring for the children. Our father's two sisters, Bertha and Bonnie, moved close by to help in any way they could.

Our father continued to work to try to hold the family together. About a year and a half later, a new mother came into the home. Our father married Arlie, who was much younger but was very motherly; immediately, there was a mutual love between her and the children. Soon, another child was born: Rita. The burden became so great caring for eight children, that all of us boys thought that this is what prompted our father to put an ad in the paper asking for a home for his two youngest children: you and Juanita.

Of course, none of the children knew that he had done this.

It seemed as though you just disappeared one day, and when we asked our father where you were, he said, "She is just visiting those nice ladies who came to see us."

After some time passed by, Sherman demanded an answer about where you really were. Father then said that he had allowed you to be adopted by a family who could provide better for you. We all got the idea that our father didn't want us to try to find you. This was when Paul and Sherman left home, saying that if he couldn't take care of you, then he could not take care of them so they would just leave. This is when Paul went into the Army, and Sherman began just traveling around—sleeping and eating where he could.

We did not know that our father was corresponding with your mother all those years, so there was absolutely no way we could even begin to look for you. It was not until 1974, when our father passed away, that I found an address that I supposed father had used to write to you all those years. That is when I wrote to you at the Princeton, Indiana, address, but it was returned and marked: "addressee unknown."

Incidentally, until you told me, I did not know that Juanita had been offered for adoption also! I think it is good that she did not know, because she would have probably felt unwanted by her own father as well as the family who came to adopt you.

As we were talking, I said to him, "Calvin, was there a little grocery store near our house in Elizabethton?"

He answered with a nod of the head.

I said, "I remember something I did when I was little. I went to the store with one of my brothers; did you ever go to the store with me?"

He chuckled and said he had gone several times with me, because I always wanted to go for walks.

I said, "Tell me if this really happened, or if I just dreamed it. We went to the store one day for some bread and milk. We always got little cans of Carnation milk—I guess we didn't have refrigeration—and on the way home, we got so hungry that you got a big rock and knocked a hole in the can, and we drank the whole can. I think we got out some bread and ate it with the milk. It was so good!"

He laughed again and said, "That is a true story, but you got one thing wrong: it was Pet milk, not Carnation!"

He continued the story. "When we got home, our mother was very upset, and of course, I was the one who got the verbal rebuke. Needless to say, we never did that again."

He was amazed that I remembered that incident that happened when I was only three years old.

Calvin and I talked and talked, scarcely stopping to eat. We did stop that evening, insisting that he take us out for a nice dinner. He went to church with us on Sunday, and after dinner, we continued our marathon. His plane did not leave until about 12:30 a.m., so LaVoy took him back to the airport so I could pull myself together for school the next day. When he left, he said he had never been so excited in all his life. He gave me a big bear hug and a kiss and said he knew we would definitely be all together soon. He said he would call and write to everyone, because he knew I was so busy with family and teaching. Hopefully, we would know by the first of October who all would be here for the big event.

It had been decided that the reunion would be at my home on Thanksgiving Day. That meant in addition to teaching, I had to get the house ready, prepare food, and plan the meals for those who were coming two or three days before the reunion. Fortunately for me, our oldest daughter, Beth, helped in planning the Thanksgiving feast and made the arrangements by ordering the food and picking up the many items that were needed.

The weeks that followed Calvin's visit were exciting and filled with so many things to do. It was difficult getting back into the classroom to teach my third graders. Almost every day, a student, parent, or colleague would ask me a question about my family, and of course, I was always thrilled to tell them what I knew. Notes, letters, and calls from my brothers and sisters came regularly—which was really a new experience. Every couple of days, an update would come from Calvin, telling me information he was getting about the reunion.

During the first week of November, I had a call from a local newspaper asking for an interview. Believe me, that had never happened before! The local CBS station wanted to tape the reunion for their evening news on Thanksgiving Day. Wow, how exciting is that?

The first article that appeared in the newspaper was in the *DeKalb News/Sun* on November 21, 1989. The reporter, Helen Ordner, came to my home and had me tell her the experience of finding my family. She wrote a beautiful story, and it was printed two days before the reunion. After the reunion, she called to tell me that the story had been chosen the "best holiday story of the season." She invited me to come to her office and see the citation she had won. I went, and she was thrilled as I told her how everything had turned out.

Derrick Hinmon, a reporter from the *Atlanta Constitution* came the day before the reunion to interview my daughter Grace, my brothers Buford and Sherman (who had already arrived), and me. This article appeared on Thanksgiving Day.

CHAPTER 8

THE REUNION

From left to right: Billie, Rita, Stella, Calvin, Juanita,
Bettye June, Sherman, Buford, Paul

What can you say about a perfect day? That is
exactly what November 23, 1989, was! It had
been preceded by three trips to the airport to
pick up Sherman and his daughter Amy, Buford
and Paul, and Paul's two daughters, Christine
and Carol. All of the other siblings were driving
from Indiana, Tennessee, and Florida. There
had been a newspaper story about finding my

siblings, and I had received many phone calls. Even though school was still in session, my dear principal had allowed me to leave early to meet my brothers at the airport each day. A very large floral arrangement had come from the school for all of us to enjoy. My sister Juanita had sent a beautiful arrangement for the table. Calvin had reserved rooms at a nearby motel for everyone so that when they left my house, they could spend the night (what was left of it) talking to each other. (And they did!)

The previous evening, my Aunt Louise and her son had come from Kennesaw, Georgia, and had enjoyed dinner with all those who had arrived. Aunt Louise was my stepmother's sister. When she had heard I was in Atlanta, she had invited us to her home several weeks before. We had spent a wonderful evening reminiscing about all the things that had gone on in my early years. She had said her sister, Arlie, had been heartbroken when I left, but she had understood and had prayed I had gone to a good Christian family who could give me what they couldn't.

The CBS station here in Atlanta called and asked if they could come and record our whole day. I was a little hesitant, because I couldn't imagine "strangers" in our midst—along with all the lights, cameras, etc.—for the whole day.

But the producer said, "We will just be like flies on the wall."

They had said they would come about 7:30 a.m. for an interview with me. That was the way my day began! After I answered what seemed to be endless questions and showed them many documents in my album, they began to bring in the remainder of cameras and set up lights all over the foyer, great room, dining room, and kitchen. We had two photographers there, and our son, Sam, was planning to video as much as he could. It was a good thing our house was large enough to accommodate all the media in addition to our large family!

About 9:00 a.m., everyone began arriving. What a joy to meet my two stepsisters, Rita and Billie from Tennessee. Billie brought what she called the Faust Family Fruit Cake. It was four layers high and delicious!

During the morning, the cameras from CBS were rolling while the reporter was interviewing the siblings as they moved about talking to all the family. There were many tears and much laughter. About 1:00 p.m., we seated ourselves at the tables for our catered Thanksgiving dinner. We began by giving thanks to the Lord for our "miracle" day and expressing gratitude to Him for making it possible for us all to be together again after fifty-one years.

After dinner, we had a short program. I welcomed everyone to our home and told them that even though I had looked for them for about twenty years, it was just a blessing from the Lord that I had found them. I explained again that it was really because of Grace and her persistence that we were together. I continue to express my appreciation to her for all her hard work. Just to think all ten of us were still able to get around after fifty-one years—especially since all of my brothers had served in the armed forces during World War II.

Then I asked each of them to give a comment about their thoughts when I called them or something about the reunion. During this time, we shed many tears of joy.

Calvin ended our day with, "Betty June, we looked for you and prayed for you for years. This has been a dream come true for all of us. We can only say: Welcome home, Betty June, we love you!"

At 6:00 p.m., we all gathered around the TV to watch channel eleven air our daily activities on the evening news. We all enjoyed it so much and it seemed we all saw different things! Fortunately, we had recorded it and replayed it many times during the evening. Almost everyone was still there to see the abbreviated version of our story on the 11:00 p.m. news segment.

It was about 1:00 a.m. when the lights went out in our home that evening. Only the Lord could have given us a day so absolutely perfect! Here are our daughter Grace's thoughts on the day's events:

Having experienced the love and security of being with my biological family all my life, it was deeply meaningful to witness my mom's blessed reunion with her many siblings after fifty-one years apart. The looks of awe and amazement, tears of joy, and lingering hugs touched even the newscasters and newspaper representatives present that day.

My husband and I, along with our first child Hannah, traveled from Virginia to be a part of this unforgettable occasion. Meeting aunts, uncles, and cousins whom I never knew existed was over-whelming. Enlightening conversations were held long into the night as the Faust siblings sought to recapture time lost and memories of years gone by. It was a day of reunion I will never forget.

The weeks that followed after the reunion remained very busy and exciting. People who had read about our reunion in the papers were calling to express their congratulations and wishing us well.

Many people asked if I was bitter that my birth father gave me up for adoption, and I always said I really never thought about being bitter, because mother explained to me that my father wanted me to have a better life than he could give me. I think my adoptive mother handled everything in such a way as to make me feel proud that I was *chosen* by them to be their daughter.

Another question I was often asked as I talked about trying to find my family was, "Aren't you afraid to find them? What if they are in jail or, even worse, you learn they had murdered some-one?" My answer was always the same — I was willing to accept whatever my siblings might be, and I had prayed about finding them. If any were in jail or in some other devastating circumstance, finding them was more important than ever so that I could tell them of God's great love and explain His plan of salvation.

My siblings continued to drop me notes, cards, and flowers. It was always such a surprise when something came from one of my brothers or sisters, because being raised as an only child never gave me that luxury. Corresponding with many nieces and nephews was also very interesting.

On my birthday (after the reunion), Calvin sent me a picture which he had had especially made. There were no photographs of just the seven of us altogether; however, he did have a picture of some of the neighborhood children, with our father holding me and a picture of the other six siblings. He took both pictures to a photographer, and he was able to very carefully put our father and me in the picture with all the siblings.

He sent an 8x10 picture to me, and on the back, he had written, "At last we are all together again after 51 years!" That picture—along with one of the reunion—hangs in my home today.

The Faust Family - Betty June is in her father's arms

CHAPTER 9

WANTED
Wanted a home for
2 small children;
Family must be Christian.

My Wonderful Siblings

After finding my family, this is what I learned about my siblings. I had prepared a questionnaire for my four brothers, two sisters and three half sisters, and they wrote their comments. I will add those at the conclusion of each sibling's information.

Paul Daniel Faust

My brother Paul was born April 26, 1919, in Knoxville, Tennessee. He was very special to the whole family. Being the oldest, the other children relied on him for many things. He was the caretaker around the house, because our father worked so many hours. He was always particularly protective of the girls. As he became older—when he would go into town for his job (helping our father at the jewelry store)—he would sometimes bring home peppermint sticks for all of us.

He was especially important to me, because he was the only one at home when our mother gave birth to me. He helped our mother and cut the cord for her.

Paul started very young helping our father in his jewelry store. This ended up being his profession: a watchmaker and diamond setter.

When I met him, I thought he looked exactly like Doc Holliday on the *Gunsmoke* TV program. He also had a very humorous side to him.

When I called him the first time (on September 9) to tell him I was his baby sister, I said "Paul, this is June."

He said, "This isn't June; it is September!"

Of course, I laughed and said, "No, Paul, this is your *baby* sister, June."

There was a long pause on the phone—I could tell he was crying.

Finally he said, "Oh, June, I never thought I would hear from you again; I am so happy!"

We continued to talk on the phone for at least an hour. He became a Christian when he was in the Army and was active in a local church.

He lived in Texas, and when he came for the reunion, he told me he would be wearing cowboy boots and a cowboy hat, and he would be waving a Texas flag. And sure enough, there he came through the Atlanta airport with his boots and hat on, waving the flag and singing, "The Eyes of Texas Are upon You." He got lots of attention at the airport, but he was easy for me to find!

His wife had passed away in the summer of 1989, and his daughter wrote me, saying that finding me seemed to give him a new lease on life.

His memories of our mother were: "very religious and many times gave her food to the kids, because food was so sparse."

His comment about the reunion: "I am overwhelmed with joy; I love you, Betty June!"

He sent many cards, notes, and letters during the rest of his life. He passed away in 2007—at the age of eighty-eight.

At the time of the reunion (1989), he had four children and eight grandchildren.

William Sherman Faust

My second brother was born September 9, 1922, in Knoxville, Tennessee. Sherman, as I called him (others called him Bill), was the tall one in the family: about 6'3". Sherman was always very special to me, because he sent me cards almost every week when I first found him and called me every other week.

As Amy, his daughter, looked at pictures of his family when he was little and saw little urchins in overalls and bare feet, she said, "Gee, Dad, you look like something from the Waltons."

He would laugh and say, not without a little pride, "No, honey, we were *real* hillbillies."

At age twelve, he began a long-lasting and enduring relationship with his Savior, the Lord Jesus Christ. He attended a tent revival and felt moved by the Spirit to accept Christ. He was baptized in the river right then and there.

Sherman told me he left home at sixteen, because, he said, "I was so upset that our father let you be adopted. I thought that if he couldn't afford to keep you, he certainly didn't need to feed me, so I left."

He traveled all over the South, sometimes traveling by boxcar and occasionally sleeping in a stranger's barn. He ended up in Mississippi and found work on a farm there. He found a nice southern family who took him in.

He also changed his name so our father couldn't find him. He took the family's last name, which was Lott, and he changed his first name to Ben. Years later, even after they had learned his true identity, he would still get Christmas cards from that family, and they were addressed to "Ben."

Somewhere along the way, he picked up cooking, and he loved it. He would make being a chef his lifelong profession. He cooked in Florida, Tennessee, Texas, and California, but his real desire was to be a preacher, and he occasionally preached for small churches. He was married for forty-four years before his beloved wife, Ruth, passed away. They had two children, two grandchildren, and one great grandchild. He was a retired chef and an ordained Baptist minister.

The last time I saw Sherman was in September 2002, before he passed away. He wanted to come to Georgia to see me—and his parents' graves in Tennessee—one more time. I was thrilled he chose to come all the way to Atlanta from Utah just to see me!

As I mentioned previously, he said his most important memory of me was when his father let another couple adopt me. He was so upset that his father would do something like that, he just left home!

His memories of our mother are of her reading her Bible and the terrible accident that took her life.

His comment on the reunion was, "Words cannot express what this means to me after all these years. It is fantastic!"

Sherman passed away in 2003 at the age of eighty-one.

I was able to share the following eulogy at his funeral on September 29, 2003:

I am Bettye Johnson, and I am from Atlanta, Georgia. I have spent my entire life in the sunny south, but I was born in the hills of Tennessee in the same family as Bill Faust. He was my second oldest brother; however, when I was four, I was adopted and separated from all my siblings.

Unfortunately, I didn't get to grow up with Bill and know him as a brother for fifty-one years, but twelve years ago, I found my family, and it was then that I was honored to have Bill come into my life.

With tears in his eyes, the first thing he said when he came to my home for a wonderful reunion was, "I thought I would never find you!" As he gave me a big bear hug and cried, he said, "You are so beautiful like I always knew you would be." (See why I loved him so?)

He told me his name was William Sherman Faust, and I said I liked the name Sherman. He said, "Well, you just call me Sherman then." So, I have always known him as Sherman. Following the reunion, he and I always exchanged birthday, Valentine, Easter, Thanksgiving, and Christmas cards—just anything that gave us an excuse to write each other. When he was no longer able to write, he would call me every three or four weeks, and we would talk and talk, sharing all about our families and their lives. Last September, he told

Amy all he wanted for his birthday was to go back East and see me, our parents' graves, and his other relatives. So, I was thrilled to have him and Amy and Lonnie come and spend a couple of days with me last September. This was the last time I saw Sherman.

But during these twelve years was when I learned who "Sherman" or "Bill" Faust really was. I found him to be a man of concern for others, a man of compassion, and a man who loved his wife, Ruth, beyond measure. Of course, he thought the sun rose and set on Amy. He was so proud of her singing, her schooling, and job. His constant concern was that she not be left alone. When she found Lonnie, he was thrilled and said, "He is just perfect for her; I know they will be happy."

Sherman was a "people person," and he spent much time telling me about the people he loved at the Senior Center, and how he would go at least once a week to have a covered dish dinner with them. He was always excited on the fourth of July when he would go to the parade, and he would talk and talk about the nice floats and bands. He would tell me about the people in his church: how much he loved them and how he liked to do things for them.

I found a little prayer not long ago, and I think this prayer is what Sherman would have prayed. It goes like this:

I do not know how long I'll live,
But while I live, Lord, let me give
Some comfort to someone in need
By smile, or nod – kind word or deed
And let me do what're I can
To ease things for my fellow man.
I want naught but to do my part
To lift a tired or weary heart
To change folks' frowns to smiles again.
Then I will not have lived in vain
And I'll care not how long I'll live
If I can give-and- give- and give!
—Sorenson

Above all, Sherman was a man who loved the Lord, served Him, and was anxious to see his Savior. So Sherman—or Bill—we love you and will remember you as a dear person God sent to us to make our lives happier and more meaningful.

Right now, I know Sherman is very happy: reunited with his lovely Ruth and sitting at the feet of his Lord Jesus Christ.

Stella Mae Faust Petersen

My sister Stella Mae was born October 4, 1924, in Knoxville, Tennessee. Stella was ten years older than I and was the one who became the "little mother" when our real mother passed away at age thirty-six. She says the memories of her childhood are of cooking, cleaning house, and babysitting.

She was the one whom I remembered, and she was the one to whom Grace wrote when trying to find my siblings. When she received the letter, she said she was so nervous she could not call me; instead, she called her brother Calvin, who also lived in Pensacola, Florida, and had him call me.

I remember Stella as always being kind and sweet to me and taking good care of me. I remember so well the last bath Stella gave Juanita and me in a big wash tub in the front yard.

Stella remembers our mother as one who was very shy, took good care of all of us, and was sick a lot.

She remembers all of the children crying and crying when our father had me adopted; as she says, "You just left us too early; we loved you so much and missed you so much."

Stella later married and had two sons and four grandchildren. Her husband passed away very young, so she raised the boys by herself. She never remarried. She lived in Pensacola, Florida.

Her comment about the reunion was: "I cannot express how grateful I am to be able to come to this reunion and, after fifty-one years, being able to spend some time with Betty June and her family. I thank God every day for being able to be with my brothers and sisters again."

I was able to visit her numerous times in Pensacola, Florida, and each time, she was so sweet and kind. She remained "sharp as a tack" until her death in 2010, when she was eighty-five.

Calvin Coolidge Faust

My third brother, Calvin, was born to Hobert and Luella Faust on November 26, 1926.

Calvin is the one who called me and introduced himself to me.

When he saw the letter which was written to Stella, he called and asked, "Is this Betty June Faust Torbett Johnson?"

When I said, "Yes."

He said, "This is Calvin Coolidge Faust, your brother."

How wonderful it was after fifty-one years to have contact with my family again!

Calvin was the organizer of the family. As I said earlier, I always thought I was organized until I met him! He was the historian of the family. He kept track of all birthdays, addresses, and happenings of all the family. He dedicated his life to Christ and was very active in many areas of the church.

Calvin had spent many years in the US Navy and was a logistician and production superintendent.

He lived with his wife, Pat, in Pensacola, Florida. They had three children and four grandchildren.

Calvin was the one who insisted I have a reunion here in my home. He was surprised but very pleased that all of the siblings could come—except one, who was ill.

The memories of his childhood were that they were depression years, and that we had only the bare necessities of life. Our mother, he said, was a very caring person and very beautiful.

His memories of me were: "You were a very active baby, and as a toddler, you were into everything!"

His reaction to the reunion was that it was: "among the very top thrills of his life."

His memorable comment at the reunion to me was: "Welcome home, Betty June; we all love you!"

Calvin passed away at the age of eighty. I was privileged to give the eulogy at his funeral on July 21, 2007:

I am Bettye Johnson, and I am Calvin's sister. Calvin is responsible for much happiness in my life for the past eighteen years, and I want to share my love and devotion to him with Pat, Richard and Robert.

Let me explain: I was adopted from the Faust family in 1938. I grew up, finished college and graduate school, married a wonderful man, and had five children and eleven grandchildren. All the time, I wondered about my birth family, and after almost twenty years of searching, it was Calvin whom I found in 1989 after fifty-one years. Actually, I didn't even know I had a brother Calvin, but my sister Stella received a letter from me through Social Security, and she had Calvin call me.

He opened up a whole new world for me. It was Calvin who told me there were ten of us children. It was Calvin who gave me all the names, phone numbers, and addresses so I could contact them immediately. In fact he said, "Call them now; if you don't call them by in the morning, I am going to; I can't keep the secret any longer!"

It was Calvin who flew up to Atlanta the next weekend to help me plan a wonderful reunion for all of us at my home. It was Calvin who rejoiced with me that all of the siblings, except one who was ill, were able to come, since they had not been together for over forty years. It was Calvin who said so lovingly at the reunion, "At long last, welcome home, Betty June."

It was Calvin who had written to me numerous times throughout the years of our separation at any address he could find for me, and it was Calvin who was always disappointed when the letters were returned to him marked "addressee unknown." It was Calvin who passed on the "family history" to me with facts, events, and pictures.

It was Calvin who, on my first birthday after we found each other, had a beautiful picture made of my father holding me superimposed over a picture of all the siblings and sent it to me with the inscription "At last we are all together again!"

It was Calvin who personally drove us up to Knoxville, Tennessee, to visit our parents' graves. It was Calvin who gave LaVoy and me a wonderful vacation in Hawaii when our son, Sam, was stationed there in the Air Force. He explained that he had missed fifty-one birthdays and Christmases with me, and that maybe this would in a small way *make up for all the times he had only thought of me and wished he could find me.*

It was Calvin who took me to the Naval Museum several times and explained to me about the huge ship he was on and what he did during the war. It was Calvin who would call me every two or three weeks "just to check on me," because as he said, "you are the baby!" This continued until we both lost our hearing and couldn't understand each other on the phone. It was Calvin who sent me a birthday card and Christmas card every year, and it was Calvin who told me he loved me just this last September when I went to visit him.

I will always remember him as a kind, loving, and gentle man who loved his Lord, his country, and his family and did everything he could for them. Calvin, I will miss you, but I know that the Lord has welcomed you into his eternal home and I know you will have no more suffering, and for that I am so thankful.

To Pat, Richard, Robert, and other family members and friends, I thank you for sharing Calvin with my family and me. Be assured of our love and prayers for you.

Buford Chadwick Faust

My fourth brother was born on August 28, 1928. Meeting Buford was such a pleasure; he was a very sharp dresser, friendly, and had a wonderful personality. He was a professional dancer and danced on the ballroom dancing channel. He often won prizes for his abilities. He was married, had two daughters, and lived in Las Vegas, Nevada.

He was in the Air Force and was a jet engine mechanic. He could do just about anything with his hands. He was a test pilot in WW II and was involved in the modifications of the B-52 bomber.

His memories of childhood were: playing with all the kids in the woods, our father coming home late after working all day trying to support us, and Stella, the oldest girl, looking after us. Our clothes were all handmade, and the boys were always looking behind stores for food.

His memory of our mother was that she was sick a lot.

Remembering me, he said, "You were so much fun to play with."

He spent most of his adult life in Las Vegas, Nevada. He married and had two daughters. When I knew him, his wife had passed away with Lou Gehrig's disease, and he was very lonely. He called me often and sent cards frequently.

His most memorable event of his life was finding me after all these years. He said it was the most wonderful event that he could remember!

The year after the reunion, the doctor told him he, too, had Lou Gehrig's disease, and that he had only a year left in which he could go and do things. The doctor also told him to do anything he wanted to do *now*.

He said, "The only thing I really want to do is go back to Georgia and see June."

So he came back to see me, and we had a wonderful week together!

Calvin and his wife came up from Pensacola and took Buford and me up to Knoxville, Tennessee, to see our parents' graves. While we were in Knoxville, we went to meet Aunt Bonnie and two of her daughters. Aunt Bonnie was the oldest of our father's living sisters. They had a marvelous "Faust Feast" waiting for us. It included many of the Faust favorite recipes, and she sent me home with copies of recipes—as well as some of their favorite home-canned items.

As it turned out, Buford had Parkinson's disease instead of Lou Gehrig's. He lived several more years but was in very poor health during that time.

In 1996, I visited him at the assisted living home in Henderson, Nevada. When we arrived on his floor, there he was at the elevator door: all dressed and waiting for me. He had no idea when I would arrive, but the nurse told me that on the day I said I would be there to see him in a couple of weeks, he had insisted on getting up every day, getting bathed and dressed, and waiting by the elevator for me. She said for months he had not been out of bed except for tests and therapy—until I told him I was coming. She said all he could talk about was June coming to see him; he told anyone who would walk by his door or come into his room.

Buford passed away in 1997 when he was sixty-nine years old. Sadly, I was unable to attend his funeral.

Frances Juanita Faust Ebbing

Juanita, as she was known, was born May 25, 1931, in Knoxville, Tennessee. Her name was one I remembered, because she and I played together most of the time—being the two youngest in the family.

She and her husband, Leo, live in Indianapolis, Indiana. They have four children and five grand-children. She says she does not remember our mother but does remember playing with me and having lots of fun.

She said that after marriage and children, meeting "June" had definitely been the most memorable event of her life. She said the reunion meant happiness and fond memories.

Juanita and I have kept in touch by sending cards and exchanging phone calls. She is now in a nursing facility in Indianapolis, Indiana.

Bettye June Faust Torbett Johnson

The following story gives the details of my birth: the seventh child born to Luella and Hobert Faust, as told to me by Paul.

"It was June 5, 1934. I will never forget that day! Aunt Bertha came and said she wanted to fix a little picnic so she could take the kids to the woods for the day. I guess she thought it would be nice to give our mother a little time to herself, knowing that the baby was due in a week or so.

I was sixteen at the time, and I decided that Calvin and Sherman could help Aunt Bertha, so I stayed home. After they left, mother went back to bed. I went into her room to be sure she was okay. She said she was okay, but that she was so distressed about bringing another child into the world when the depression was causing so many people to lose their jobs, and basically, we were in the throes of poverty.

She also told me that the baby had become very still, and that it wouldn't be long—she was sure. She asked me to stay close by, since no one else was home.

Shortly, I heard her walking around in the bedroom. I went to check on her again, and she was gathering towels and a basin for water. The pains grew worse as she gasped for breath. I asked her what I could do, and she said to just be with her, and she would tell me how I could help.

It seemed like I watched our mother suffer for hours. The pains seemed to come very quickly and lasted longer and longer. Finally, I saw your tiny head appear, and then I heard a cry. She told me to cut the cord for her. I didn't even know what a cord was, and I was shaking all over!

I took you and covered you with a blanket and showed you to our mother. I remember she said that you were so beautiful, and I surely agreed with her. Then she turned over and fell into a deep sleep. I just couldn't believe that I had actually helped you come into this world! I was still shaking so badly, and I remember I thought it was the biggest mess I had ever seen!

When the kids came home, they were all excited about their day in the woods: eating, picking berries, and picking flowers to bring home to Mother. But when they saw me holding you, they just stood there and stared. Stella complained that I always got to have all the fun and do special things. But she had no idea of what I had been through! I certainly wouldn't have called it fun, but I was so glad I was able to help mother when she needed me. All of them just "oohed" and "aahed" over you as you stared at them with those big brown eyes.

After all the commotion, supper was finally ready, and the children sat down to eat. Just then, our father could be heard coming up the steps on the front porch. He had come home early, knowing that the baby was due at any time.

All the kids wanted to run and tell him, but Aunt Bertha said I should tell him, because I had a part in your birth.

I remember: I picked you up and went to the door and said, "Hi; meet your new daughter."

After Paul related this story to me, he said, "See why I love you more than all the others?"

Rita Ann Foust

I do not have much information about my half-sisters, except the dates of their births. Since their mother's maiden name was Foust (with the "o" spelling), they chose to retain that spelling for their last name.

Rita was born March 2l, 1937, to Hobert and Arlie Faust (our stepmother) in Clinton, Tennessee. She has lived most of her life in the home where her mother grew up in Lake City, Tennessee.

When Buford came from Las Vegas to see me, Calvin came from Pensacola and took us up to see our parents' graves in the Washington Pike Cemetery in Knoxville, Tennessee. While in the area, we stopped by to see Rita. She was very kind and invited us in for lemonade.

Born just before I was adopted, I thought Rita was a cute little baby. I remember Arlie wrapping her in blankets and taking her out for walks.

Rita spent many years driving a school bus.

Linda Estelle Foust

Linda, my second half-sister, was born on April 6, 1939, in Pasadena, Texas. She spent most of her life in Las Vegas and Glendora, California. She had a little boy, Terry, whom my brother Sherman adopted and raised as his own child. She is the only member of my family whom I have not met, as she was ill when we had our reunion. She lives in Glendora, California, and we have corresponded occasionally.

Billie Lee Foust Leon

Billie was born on February 10, 1940, in Pasadena, Texas. She was married and has three children. She lived most of her married life in Tampa, Florida. After her husband, Pete, passed away, she moved to Lake City, Tennessee, to be near her sister Rita.

I was flabbergasted when I learned that for over thirty years Billie had been living just a few miles from my husband's parents in Tampa, Florida. LaVoy and I and our family had visited his home every year! Oh, had I only known…!

CHAPTER 10

WANTED
Wanted a home for
2 small children;
Family must be Christian.

My Father and Aunt Bertha

In February, 1990, a reporter called from *Woman's World Magazine* to tell me they would like for me to go Pensacola, Florida, so they could interview Calvin, Stella, and me for an article they wanted to run in the "American Family" section of the magazine. They paid all expenses, and Calvin, Stella, and I had a wonderful time together. This was the first time I had been to see Calvin, and it was a delight to be in his home and see how he lived. He gave me more information about our father.

One of the interesting things was that in 1953, when my father moved to North Carolina, he had to have a duplicate birth certificate made, because his original had been misplaced.

On the application, he had to list many official pieces of paperwork. One was to list the birth of a child. He listed: "Birth Certificate of daughter #D-331549-Tennessee, born 6/5/34."

They all thought it very strange that he would list my birth date; after all, he had nine other children. Why would he have done this? My brothers thought perhaps it was because he may have felt guilty all his life that he had let me go. Who knows? Oh, how I wish I could have talked to him before he passed away!

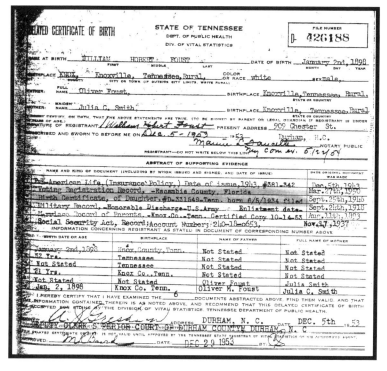

My father's duplicate birth certificate, listing my birth

Calvin told me that Paul, Sherman, and he had cleaned out our father's apartment when he died. When they went into the bedroom, they found a 20x16 portrait on the wall across from the bed. It was a picture of a little dark-haired, brown eyed girl holding a cat.

They all looked at each other and shook their heads. Why would their father have a picture like that on his wall? They took the picture off the wall, and on the back was a note that said: "My beautiful June—how I love her!"

Calvin gave the picture to me and said, "Our father really loved you and was concerned about you all his life."

Also among his belongings was a picture album of all the pictures my mother had sent to him over the years. Calvin said it was carefully placed between his bed and the bedside table. It was a strange feeling to see those pictures again, knowing that my adoptive mother had sent them to him so many years before.

The article appeared in the June issue of *Woman's World Magazine*. The author, Sarah Widner, did an excellent job on the story. It was very interesting to see the different ways the reporters approached the story.

The following summer, another article appeared in the *Voice of the Alumni*, the monthly publication of my alma mater, Bob Jones University, in Greenville, South Carolina. After this appeared, I heard from many of my classmates that I had not heard from since college. They were all very excited for me and said that in college, they just remembered me as a "normal kid."

On my birthday in June, 1990, Aunt Bertha and Uncle Harry baked a wonderful cake for me and sent it overnight mail so I could enjoy a Faust cake. Her note said, "After fifty-one years, you certainly deserve a birthday cake baked by a Faust."

Aunt Bertha became dear to our family. She would call frequently, and we would enjoy sharing what was going on in our lives. We visited her several times when we went to Phoenix, Arizona, to see our daughter Pattye and her family. I discovered that she liked crafts and that her hobbies were much like mine: quilting, knitting, crocheting, and cross-stitching.

Pattye and I made a special trip to Sedona in 1996 when we went to give a ninetieth birthday party for her. She had said she was entering her second childhood, so we had all the hats, balloons, and whistles as though she were a little girl. She loved it!

Bettye June and Aunt Bertha

After Aunt Bertha became ill, Pattye would check on her through a friend of Aunt Bertha's in Sedona. The last time Pattye went to see her, she insisted on giving me the only quilt she had ever made. She made it during WWII; she said it took forever! She was always amazed that anyone could make more than one quilt in his or her lifetime! She told Pattye that she could never get over the fact her brother Hobert had let me be adopted, and that for fifty-one years, she had prayed for me and thought about me, and she wanted me to have a Faust heirloom. Pattye graciously accepted it and brought it to me. It is absolutely beautiful—appliquéd and hand-quilted—and is something my heirs and I will always cherish. Today, it hangs on a wall in my home.

These are Pattye's comments on her visits with Aunt Bertha and Uncle Harry:

Whew! What a pair they were! They were so much fun and such a delight to get to know in their last few years of life. They would incessantly tease each other. I'll never forget Aunt Bertha telling Uncle Harry he was as slow as "Merry Christmas." Uncle Harry's birthday was Christmas Day, so I guess she was right.

Aunt Bertha's Quilt

We met Aunt Bertha and Uncle Harry for the first time on Thanksgiving, 1989. Mom had recently found her biological family, and they were having a big reunion in Atlanta. We lived too far to attend (Phoenix) but were delighted to find out there was extended family in Sedona, Arizona. We made our plans to celebrate the holiday with Mom's newly found aunt and uncle.

That first visit was one of several over the years—until they passed away. They lived in a small home on a hill in Sedona. The view from their front window was breathtaking. The beautiful red rocks of Sedona and the unique desert landscaping of flowers and cacti created a gorgeous panorama. We would sit for hours in their front room and chat about anything and everything. Sometimes, I would play their ancient little organ, and Aunt Bertha would sing old songs from the forties and fifties. Uncle Harry would cook a delicious dinner for us—including his famous cake: "Harry's Wallbanger Cake." Usually I don't care much for non-chocolate desserts, but Uncle Harry's cake was amazing.

Every visit also included Aunt Bertha and Uncle Harry's two Pomeranian dogs. They had a loud, high-pitched bark, and boy, would they bark! Aunt Bertha and Uncle Harry loved these dogs: even though they were high maintenance. I also remember our children always looked forward to the boxes of chocolate-covered Oreos that seemed to find their way into our car—and mouths—as we drove back to Phoenix. Aunt Bertha and Uncle

Harry were very generous people. I always worried that people would take advantage of them.

I look back at those years (the early nineties) and our time with Aunt Bertha and Uncle Harry as a treasure and as our closest connection to Mom's biological family. They were a joy to know and love.

CHAPTER 11

GOD TAKES CARE OF HIS OWN

My adoptive mother always said I lived a "charmed life." I really never knew what she meant; but as I look back, I can see many miracles, which at the time seemed to be simply routines of everyday life.

One example that often comes to mind happened shortly after my mother passed away. She and Aunt Gertrude had sold the house and farm in Indiana but had insisted on keeping the oil rights throughout their lifetime. They moved near my husband and me in Avondale Estates, Georgia, so Mother could see her only grandchildren grow up. Mother had told me that in her will she was leaving everything to Aunt Gertrude, because there would be no one left to take care of her. I certainly understood.

About six weeks after Mother's death, I received a large check from the oil company. (The old oil wells had begun producing oil again.)

When I asked Aunt Gertrude about it, she said, "Oh, that is a mistake; all the oil money is supposed to come to me."

Then, when I called the oil company and explained the situation, I was told no mistake had been made—that they had my name on their records as Mother's adopted daughter, and that I was to get the money, but that they would research the records to verify it all.

Several weeks later, I received a letter explaining that I was right: her will had indicated the money was to go to Aunt Gertrude. However, they learned that, legally, they could not do that, because I had been adopted, and the law stated that Mother could not disown me, which is what she would be doing if the money went to Aunt Gertrude. They reminded me that I could do whatever I wanted to with the money, but the oil company checks would continue to be sent to me.

This all came at a time when our three daughters were enrolled in a private Christian school, which considerably increased the demands on our family's budget. Knowing what Mother's wishes had been, I knew I must send the checks from the oil company on to Aunt Gertrude. However, realizing our family's needs, Aunt Gertrude very graciously had me keep that first check!

We obviously saw this as God's way of taking care of His own, and it reminded me immediately of the heritage we have as Christians. Once we accept the Lord as our Savior, He will never disown us.

Romans 8:38–39b promises: "For I am persuaded, that neither death, nor life, nor angels, nor principalities, nor powers, nor things present, nor things to come...shall separate us from the love of God, which is in Christ Jesus our Lord."

Epilogue

I have wanted to write this book ever since the wonderful reunion with all my siblings in 1989. The joy of staying in touch with them for the past twenty-plus years and the privilege of delivering eulogies for two of my beloved brothers cannot be measured.

I pray these pages will be an inspiration to others who are searching for family members and will perhaps motivate some who have hesitated to begin the search. The satisfaction you will experience in the new relationships will far outweigh any time, money, or effort you might expend.

I can only say that my life has been blessed beyond measure—abundantly, above all, and beyond anything I could have ever imagined. Romans 8:28, my life's verse, continues to strengthen and encourage me through the everyday trials of life: "And we know that all things work together for good to them that love God, to them who are the called according to His purpose."

To God be the glory!

You may contact Bettye with questions or comments at: TheWantAd1938@gmail.com

Made in the USA
San Bernardino, CA
01 May 2014